MW01488561

That's How It Is
Down Here

IF IT'S NOT ONE THING, IT'S ANOTHER

DR. G. CALVIN MCCUTCHEN, SR.

CROSSBOOKS

CrossBooks™
A Division of LifeWay
One LifeWay Plaza
Nashville, TN 37234
www.crossbooks.com
Phone: 1-866-768-9010

Author photo by Don Thompson

First published by CrossBooks 09/04/2014

ISBN: 978-1-4627-5244-7 (sc)
ISBN: 978-1-4627-5243-0 (e)

Contents

Dedicated to My Wife
Mrs. Adelene Dixon McCutchen
Gone But Not Forgotten

Preface

A well known evangelist is quoted in an English publication of having told the following story in one of his campaigns. He said, "I have a friend who during the depression lost his job, a fortune, a wife and a home, but believe it or not, he held on to his faith in God – the only thing he had left.

One day he stopped to watch some men doing stone work on a huge church building. One of them was chiseling a triangular piece of rock. "What are you going to do with that?" his friend asked. The workman said, "Do you see that little opening way up there near the spire?" Well I'm shaping this down here so that it will fit in up there."

Tears filled his eyes as he walked away. God had spoken through the workman to explain the ordeal through which he was passing.

Some of you who are reading this book may be going through some difficult times. Perhaps you are in a great deal of pain and physical disability. This outward man seems to be perishing. Yet if you are a child of God, you should not despair, nor faint, for all these things are from the loving hand of our Heavenly Father who is shaping us down here so we will fit in up there.

All of us live in houses of clay, which will soon return to the dust. Yet it is a blessing to know as God work upon the pliable putty of our human frailty, it can result for us in "an eternal weight of glory," if through the process our inward man is renewed and shaped more perfectly according to His divine will.

Keep this in mind as you read these from the heart of one who has had his share of ups and downs, trials and tribulations, perplexities and problems, that God is but shaping us down here so that we will fit in up there.

Other thoughts are given in this book. Anyone can serve the Lord when everything is going great. But keep this in mind, we cannot be victorious if we do not have anything to be victorious over. Everyone lives closer to God when trouble come than at any other time. Any experience that draws us closer to God is a blessing. We cannot know the power of God in our lives without trouble.

Keep this in mind – God is bigger than any problem we will ever have. All the hardships of the world may wear you pretty thin. But they won't hurt you one lease bit unless you let them in.

Navigating Through the Sea of Trouble

*"And when the disciples saw Him walking
On the sea they were troubled."
~ Matthew 14:26 ~
(NKJV)*

This incident the Devine Spirit has prompted me to share with you tonight is lifted from a midnight scene.

It was the night following our Lord's feeding of the five thousand with a lad's lunch of three fish and five loaves of bread. The day had been extremely busy for our Christ. The crowd had pressed him -- He had healed them and taught them. When it was late in the evening He had fed them and sent them away quietly to their homes.

In the meantime He had sent the disciples across the lake in a small boat. When the people were gone, He turned to the mountain to spend the night in prayer. As His disciples made their way to the distant shore there arose a great storm. The sea became mountainous with billows. These disciples found themselves rowing very hard in their attempt to make it to the distant shore.

With all their sincere efforts they were beaten by the wind and the waves, trying to match their skill and strength against the power of the wind and the waves.

The Bible gives us to believe that one by one they yielded to the seemingly inevitable and gave up the fight. But one thing that can be said about our Lord, He has a tendency to step right in when He is needed most.

During the last watch of the night, our Lord found His disciples exhausted, dispirited and ready to die. Mark tells us in his account of this same incident, he saw their strength break under the force of the storm. He saw their hearts filled with fear and anxiety. He saw them seemingly facing death, clinging to the last straw of hope.

Our Lord, who had watched them from the mountain peak, came to them walking on the water. The text reads, "and when the disciples saw Him walking on the sea they were troubled."

One thought comes to mind. Our Lord's miracles are exciting and intoxicating, but when we are cut off from Christ and thrown into the thick of life's fierce battles the question is, 'what does Christ mean to us?'

Their admiration of Christ seemed limited to His physical presence. They forgot that He was able to save them even when they were away from Him. This was a lesson that could not be taught neither by precept nor by miracles but had to be taught by a storm. A lesson that could not be written in books, but had to be written in real experience.

The text reads, "and when the disciples saw Him walking on the sea, they were troubled."

Pray with me while I talk from this all important subject --

NAVIGATING THROUGH THE SEA OF TROUBLE.

In this life it is ours to be confronted with all kinds of trouble.

I call our attention first of all to **NATURAL TROUBLES.** I repeat, these disciples were troubled with the forces of nature and their own wellness. Such trouble, as all men, the saved and the unsaved alike, ours is a world that's full of trouble. It is a world where storms destroy the property and lives of the good as well as the bad.

Ours is a land where sickness is not confined to the unbelieving only. Job would tell us that it invades the ranks of the holiest and best as well. Trouble and trials comes to us all.

The whole world joins in the cry of the throng that crucified Christ saying, 'He trusted in God, let Him deliver Him now, He saved others, Himself He cannot save.'

There are natural troubles. Troubles that comes to saints and sinners alike. Nowhere does the promise of salvation give one a passport through this world of sorrow. Our faith will be tried, persecution will arise, and even sickness and death can be expected for us all. There are natural troubles.

Then there are **IMAGINARY TROUBLES** -- This kind of trouble was very much like what those disciples had that night on the sea. When Christ appeared they thought, 'He was a spirit, a ghost coming to torment them more.' This was because they were looking for trouble. Had they been looking for Christ and expecting Him at any minute, His appearance to them would have been their greatest joy. The fact that they were looking for trouble, they made trouble out of everything.

How easy it is to find slights and causes for injuries in anyone if you are looking for those things.

I have mentioned **NATURAL TROUBLES and IMAGINARY TROUBLES** -- let's look at **SATANIC TROUBLES.**

Jesus asked His disciples, 'wherefore didst thou doubt.' These disciples were beaten and whipped because they doubted our Lord. They were full of fears and misgivings because they doubted.

Why did they doubt?

They had seen enough of His miracles. They knew enough about God's power to help. Why did they doubt.

Satan caused it. He made them forget the power of an Almighty God. Doubting is the chief weapon of the devil. I think I need to tell us that the world is full of evidence that our God is able, but Satan has blinded the eyes and made deaf the ears and dulled the senses of so many that the spell of doubt can only be broken by a closer walk with God.

We have mentioned natural trouble, imaginary trouble, satanic trouble -- consider last:

DIVINE TROUBLES -- These are the ones that grow out of our relationship to Jesus Christ. Not troubles He has caused but trouble we bring ourselves because of His absence.

Note -- as soon as Jesus came, their troubles vanished. The storm ceased and their problem was solved.

I ought to tell us the absence of Christ always intensifies our troubles. Sorrow is bad enough, but it is worse when we have to bear it without the comforting presence of Christ. His presence will solve all problems.

If our life is stormy, give Him the rightful place in all the details and peace and quietness will reign. Our greatest need is Jesus.

As I make an effort to close this message, permit me to tell you that our greatest need is Jesus. It is always too soon to quit, to surrender to despair.

This incident was reported some time ago in a Los Angeles newspaper. A young man jumped to his death from a window of a downtown hotel.

Behind his suicide lay an amazing, pathetic story. He had run up a batch of bills, including the hotel bill where he was staying, without any money to pay.

Driven by pressure this young man took what he believed to be his only way out. He had wired his brother concerning his plight.

The real tragedy was the moment he took his suicidal jump, there was waiting in the lobby of the hotel, sent by his brother, enough money to cover all the bills he had made.

No matter how dark things look, no matter how insurmountable the problem may seem, nothing is too hard for God.

He alone can

+ mend a broken heart
+ cleanse a sin sick soul
+ give one victory over Satan
+ lighten your burden no matter how heavy
+ remove all your doubts and fears no matter how many.

No one can do what Christ can do. He can transform one's nights into days. He can change burdens into blessings. He can transform weakness into strengths. He can change difficulties into-delights and one's gloom into glory.

What a friend we have in Jesus.

In Him we have someone to care.

In closing, let me say folk become victims of the storm because they --

Stop reading the Word
Stop attending church
Neglect their prayer life
Allow their ego to get in the way
Yield to the wrong spirit
Refuse to take advantage of God's refuge.

Only one refuge to keep one safe from the storms of life -- JESUS CHRIST. He is a Rock in a weary land and a shelter from the storms of life.

I've found this out about Jesus --

He may not eliminate the storms, but He will give you grace to withstand them.

He will not divert the storms from coming your way. He will hold your hand and protect you through them.

He will not weaken the storms, He will give you the needed strength to overcome them.

He will not simply remove the storms, He will give you peace in the midst of them,

He will not prevent the storms from coming your way -- if you trust Him in the midst of the storms -- which is the better.

In Life's Problems God Has A Plan

"In the world you will have tribulation;
But be of good cheer, I have overcome the world."
~ John 16:33 ~
(NKJV)

On September 11, 2001, most of us began our day like any other. But by the day's end our lives were changed forever, as we watched the news reports recounting the terrorist attack on our country that killed over 3,000 people.

On Monday, September 10, 2001 there were people fighting against praying in schools. On Tuesday, September 11 you would have been hard pressed to find a school where someone was not praying.

On Monday we thought we were secure — on Tuesday we learned better. On Monday, people were fighting the Ten Commandments on government property. These people said "God help us" all while thinking "Thou shalt not kill." On Monday some kids had solid families — on Tuesday they were orphans.

During the months that followed that horrific devastation, we wept with the many as they told their story about the loss of their loved ones that day. Their pain and our nation's pain will be with us for years and years to come.

Life is full of twists and turns.

Life, as many of us know it, consists of many ups and downs. Throughout this nation and even in our city right now, many people are experiencing their own world-collapsing crisis.

A young man's heart which had become a receptacle for love for a certain young lady is now filled with pain he could never have imagined because she said no to his marriage proposal.

There's that family that has had no income for months. The unemployment check has run out, and there's no prospect for a job.

A young athlete who has spent 15 years working toward his dream of playing professional ball hears the surgeon saying, "Your knee injury is beyond repair."

A 40 year old man has just walked out of the doctor's office in a dazed fog is still trying to make sense of the deadly prognosis he's just heard.

A wife said goodbye to her husband as he boarded a flight to Boston on September 11 — two hours later, he and over 3,000 others are dead.

I repeat — life is full of many twists and turns.

Throughout this nation and even in our own city, many are experiencing their own world-collapsing crisis.

Your crisis, nor mine, may or may not make the nightly news. But to us, it is just as painful. There are so many life crushing events that happen to people you and I know daily, like the loss of a good job, the loss of a spouse through divorce or because of death, mental illness in your family, being robbed or victimized in other ways.

Sometimes the bad things happen to us along with the good. Painful challenges come to us all and why do they come? I would say they come just to test our faith in God. The late Dr. E. V. Hill once said -- "We had no trouble before we were born and we will have none when we are gone." The Master -- it's in the fine print -- said, "In this world you will have tribulation... and

That's How It Is Down Here.
If It's Not One Thing It's Another.

Three things I'm going to say about this tonight and I'm through!

I. FIRST, HUMAN LIFE IS ORDINARILY A LITTLE ELSE THAN A COLLECTION OF DISAPPOINTMENTS.

There are reasons for this.

God had a wonderful plan for each of our lives. And we have our own plan. We try to by-pass His plan. We concoct a plan of our own. When we try to make it on our own, we experience a series of disappointments. God knows what's best for us.

Many a person there is who sought to be a farmer and ended up a mechanic. Likewise, there are those who started out to be a lawyer, and ended up a preacher and later pastor a church.

If It's Not One Thing It's Another.

Success in one's life depends upon one's motive. A rabbit for the most part can out-run a dog. The rabbit is running for his life, the dog is running for his dinner.

If you are in life's race only for your meal ticket, you will not put quite as much energy into your running as you would if your ambition is deeper and more serious.

Human life as we know it is a little less than a collection of disappointments. There are things we bump into and things that bump into us. But -- **That's How It Is Down Here. If It's Not One Thing It's Another.**

That brings me to my next thought.

II. <u>THIS LIFE WE ARE CONFRONTED WITH HAS PROBLEM AFTER PROBLEM.</u>

On a busy highway, while another was driving, I watched a small sparrow soar from the top of a utility pole. It glided across the road into the path of a moving vehicle. The injured bird was knocked to the pavement where it sought to evade the wheels of this fast moving car.

Its efforts were hopeless -- the traffic was too heavy, the automobile was too fast, and the driver was too pre-occupied. That sparrow (that was noticed by God) who attended its funeral, when it fell, was to us but a victim of a hectic mechanized society. In this life we are confronted with one problem after the other. Nationally we have a problem.

Our President appears to be bent on going to war -- and there are demonstrations for peace not war all over our land.

There is an economic crisis which affects the services in our city, county, state and nation. There is a lot of downsizing in major corporations which have resulted in a shortage of jobs.

Since we met here last -- I've had my own set of problems. My brother died in Louisville, Kentucky and one month and one day later I went back to also preach the funeral of his wife. And only a few weeks ago -- my son while changing a flat tire in a residential neighborhood -- someone attempted to rob him of his little paycheck. When he refused, he was shot in the head and left to die.

In this life we are confronted with one problem after the other. Get one problem solved -- and there are two to take its place.

By the time you get your car paid for it's falling apart. If it's not a set of new tires, the brakes need to be replaced. If it's not the transmission, it's the wheels that need alignment. If it's not the car it's the house. If it's not the roof that leaks, it's the termites eating away the foundation. By the time you get your taxes paid, the insurance is due.

If it's not the heating unit that needs repairing, it's the air condition compressor that must be replaced.

Even the elements of nature get to us.

If it's not too hot -- it's too cold. If it's not snowing -- it's raining and 19 drops of water can cause 20 Baptists to stay at home.

Then two physical bodies may be as beautiful as the starry skies, but as fading as a summer flower. If it's not your eyesight -- it's your hearing. If it's not your lungs -- it's your kidneys. If it's not your hair falling out -- it's your teeth that need fixing. If it's not your back that's hurting -- it's your feet that's giving you trouble. And if arthritis don't stop us from walking -- laryngitis will stop us from talking.

If It's Not One Thing, It's Another.

I have said two things. First, Human Life is ordinarily little less than a series of disappointments. Secondly, I said, in this life we are confronted with one problem after the other.

My final thought is this:

III.   ADVERSITY IS NOT OUR GREATEST PROBLEM.

It is not our problems that mess us up. It's how we deal with them which is so important.

All of us complain occasionally. Most of us complain frequently. Some folk complain all the time.

We complain about the weather, about politics, about football, the price of everything, our taxes and some about religion.

Whatever our complaint, however justified or not, the problem is rarely removed by our complaining.

The weather keeps on changing, the political parties remain unchanged, football teams still win or lose -- and taxes remain our annual pain.

But I think I need to tell us -- in every aspect of life, even in tragedy's darkest night -- the light of God is always there. We need only to look and believe.

The Master told His disciples -- when they were trying to solve some of the mysteries of life -- "When it comes to worry -- Don't do it." -- "Have faith in God."

Adversity is not our greatest enemy. How we deal with them is so important. We are serving a God who will bring you through it to get you to it!

A frog once happened into a deep rut on a country road, and though his friends tried desperately to get him out -- they were unsuccessful and finally left him there in deep despair. The next day one of these friends was hopping along and met the frog he had left in the rut the day before.

"I'm surprised to see you" the frog said. "I thought you were unable to get out of that rut."

"I couldn't get out" said the other frog, "but a truck came along and I had to!"

Only a fable -- but it illustrates the fact that necessity often overcomes the impossible.

All of us fall into ruts of adversity -- and if we aren't careful, we will become prisoners of these ruts we find ourselves in. What we need is determination -- a compelling reason -- faith enough to jump out and our problem for the most part is solved.

With determination, with faith and a compelling reason -- all obstacles and ruts of life's highway turn into stepping-stones that can lead us to ultimate achievement.

The message of the cross is not just that the impossibilities of death's darkness have been overcome, but rather that the promises of life have been made available to all.

As the disciples of long ago - we each stand at the foot of the cross looking up. And now Christ asks each of us the question, **where do you go from here?** I've got to close work here!

There's a song that keeps ringing in my ears -- saying I'm a living testimony -- I could have been dead and gone -- I thank the Lord I'm still alive.

The man I work for asked me to work a little while longer.

Many of my friends have punched their clocks -- gone home. There was J. C. Jackson, C. L. West, Calvin K. Stalnaker, T. Oscar Chappell, Sr., Norman Kerry, Sr., and Samuel Austin. Most recently Frederick Sampson, Emmanuel Scott Sr., E. V. Hill, J. H. Alexander, J. J. Jones, T. C. Morris, L. L. Tisdale, Ervin Ruthe, M. D. Johnson, J. H. Dotson -- all have punched their clocks and gone home.

I'm going to work here a little while longer.

Trouble – no one likes it, but no one is ever completely successful in avoiding it. One way or another, trouble seems to be a fact of life. Trouble has no age preference. It invades the life of the young person as well as the life of the old.

Trouble has no respect of gender, race or social circle. At one time or another trouble comes into the lives of the famous and the unknown, the rich and the poor.

You may think that you will never face trouble. But if you stay around long enough, trouble will come knocking at your door. The Bible says, "Many are the afflictions of the righteous, but the Lord delivers him out of them all."

**That's How It Is Down Here.
If It's Not One Thing It's Another.**

From Our Problems to His Promises

"Many are the afflictions of the righteous,
But the Lord delivers him out of them all."
~Psalm 34:9~
NKJV

What would life be without some sort of trouble? Trouble and trials in this life are as common to man as scales are to fish and they are as sure as the rainy day after you have washed and polished your car. And I am thoroughly convinced that trouble is one of the penalties everyone pays for being a member of the human race.

Calvin N. Nash, in his book, "The Trying of Your Faith" says, "There is good trouble and bad trouble." There is no dark path in your life that God can't shine His light on and any experience that is ours that brings us closer to God – is good trouble.

We have some big big problems, but we are serving a big big God.

Many are the afflictions of the righteous, but the Lord delivers him out of them all. He keeps proving Himself to me. My car is now 8 years old. It has almost 150,000 miles on the speedometer. During the past two years, to keep that car on the road, I have experienced all kinds of trouble, none solicited. Some expected, some unexpected.

The problems have gone from fuel injection system, water pump, alternator, heater core unit, to the replacing of the radio stereo cassette player.

I even had to replace the over-hang in the ceiling, and they had to remove the rear window to do it. And I haven't even mentioned the radiator and a new set of tires.

I've had so much car trouble during the past two years that I could ask the Lord, "Why am I picked out to be picked on?"

But then it comes to me like the peal of a bell on a clear night. **That's How It Is Down Here. If It's Not One Thing It's Another.**

The Bible says, "Many are the afflictions of the righteous, but the Lord delivers him out of them all."

I'm not going to keep you long tonight. There are three things I'm going to say with the Divine Spirit's help and I'm through.

First, I think I need to tell us if you find a path that has no trouble, you will also find that it leads to nowhere.

Paul Harvey said, "You can always tell when you are on the road to success, it is up-hill all the way."

The only peaceful, trouble-free place I know that is on this earth is the cemetery.

We had no trouble before we were born and we will have none when we are gone. But as Dr. Caesar Clark says,

"From the launching to the landing, you will encounter some trouble along the way."

That's How It Is Down Here.
If It's Not One Thing, It's Another.

We are all church folk here tonight. Let's talk about church trouble.

Some years ago, I co-authored a book with Dr. J. van Alfred Winsett, Pastor, Ebenezer Baptist Church, Pittsburgh, Pennsylvania. We called it, "The Pastor's Headaches."

In that little book we pointed out that in most churches there are three groups. There are the shirkers, the jerkers and a very few workers. We also said in some churches there are but two groups, the runners and the other group that spend their time blocking the runners.

We also agreed that the chief trouble in any church is you and I who are in it. Trouble apparently comes to us as church fails to keep our religion from getting rusty.

I talk to a lot of preachers in this city, state and nation. Some of us are in trouble and don't even know it.

Preachers, you're in trouble when:

The only raise you get is the elevation of the congregation's hands to vote you out.

The congregation thinks walking in the light means attending day-time services only. You ask for a raise and they build the pulpit two steps higher.

On this journey down here, expect some kind of trouble. It's an up-hill journey. If you are on a road and find no trouble, rest assured it's a road to nowhere.

Our next thought is this – trouble like crosses comes in many shapes and sizes.

It could be a flat tire on an expressway when you are already late for an urgent appointment.

It could be remembering today an appointment you missed yesterday.

It could be a personal injury accident in which you are at fault and your liability insurance just expired because the premium you failed to pay.

It could be a mortgage payment past due, and you have no job and very little left in the savings account.

If It's Not One Thing, It's Another.

As soon as you get one problem solved, whether it be at home, on the job, at church – then comes another sometimes two more to take its place.

By the time you get your car paid for, it's falling apart. If it's not the tires, it's the brakes. If it's not the transmission it's the wheels that need an alignment.

Get your car problems solved, house problems begins – the roof leaks. Get the roof replaced then you discover the termites are destroying the foundation.

By the time the taxes are paid the insurance is due. If it's not the furnace that need fixing, it's the air condition that need to be replaced. If it's not the paint, it's the plumbing.

If It's Not One Thing, It's Another.

Even the elements causes us trouble. If it's not too hot, it's too cold. This year El Nino caused snow storms in one area, floods in another. If it's not a storm watch, it's a flood watch or a tornado watch.

If It's Not One Thing, It's Another.

Our bodies also get into the act. They may appear to be as beautiful as the starry sky but they are as fading as a summer flower.

If it's not your eyesight, it's your hearing. If it's not your lungs, it's your kidneys. If it's not your hair that's falling out, your teeth need fixing.

If it's not your back that's hurting you, it's your feet that's giving you trouble. If it's not too much weight, it's too little weight. If arthritis don't stop you from walking, laryngitis will stop you from talking. If you don't have a cold, you are burning up with a fever.

That's How It Is Down Here.
If It's Not One Thing, It's Another.

Let me go back to church.

If it's not the program, it's the budget. Get one Auxiliary built up, another falls down. Trouble, like crosses comes in many shapes and sizes. But,

That's How It Is Down Here.
If It's Not One Thing, It's Another.

This brings me to my final thought –

It is this – Although trouble down here is a fact of **life**, let's not confuse the facts of life with the acts of God. Life is never fair, but God is still good. God is good all the time, and all the time God is good.

Before closing let me offer a few suggestions, how best to live in times like these and in a world like ours.

First, I would suggest that our focus must shift from our problems to God's promises. Adversity is not our greatest enemy.

It's not our problems that mess us up. It's how we deal with them. For instance, Abraham Lincoln was raised in poverty. Yes, he became the 16th President of the United States.

Franklin Delano Roosevelt was stricken with paralysis, but he served as President 20 years longer, and did more good than any President before or since. If you can take it, you can make it.

Our focus must shift from our problems to His promises. Once this is done, I would suggest that you would stand on the promises of God.

God brings us through it to get us to it!

Be ye steadfast, unmovable, always abounding in the work of the Lord.

I thank God for my mountains, and my valleys. I've seen the lightening flashing, and I've heard the thunder roll.

Stand on the promises. God can –

Turn turmoil into peace –
Turn misery into glory –
Turn burdens into blessings –
Turn trouble into triumphs.

Finally, I would suggest that we let the Lord fix it for us. Whatever He fixes stays fixed.

If you hold to His hands and live by His Commands – if you're lost, don't stay lost.

When you reach the river, the road is going to change.

Living With Persistent Perplexity

"From the Jews five times I received forty stripes minus one. Three times I was beaten with rods; once I was stoned, three times I was shipwrecked; a night and a day I have been in the deep. In journeys often, in perils of waters, in perils of robbers, in perils of my own countrymen, in perils of the Gentiles, in perils in the city, in perils in the sea, in perils among false brethren;"
~ II Corinthians 11:24-26 ~
NKJV

Allow me to introduce this message tonight by sharing two stories Paul Harvey tells, to prove this one fact – which some folk have more than their share of bad things that happen to them.

He tells of a man who after finishing an out of town errand, discovered his car stopped and would not restart because it was out of gas.

He was told he could find a gas station about a mile and a half away. He took his gas can from the trunk of his car and trudged the distance to the gas station in the sweltering heat.

The attendant filled his two-gallon can and he lugged it all the way back and poured the gas into the tank. When he tried to unlock the car door, it wouldn't open.

Just then he noticed an identical car parked a short distance away. That was his car. He had poured his two gallons of gasoline in the tank of a stranger's car.

There was but one thing left for him to do, to get home before the day was over, he had to start all over again.

Paul Harvey also tells about a man who had so many things to go wrong in his life, he decided he would end it by leaping from a five story building.

He jumped but he landed on the top of a man driving a convertible. The fall killed the driver of the car and the man who jumped survived the fall, and was charged with murder.

It is a known fact that some folk seem to have more than their share of bad things that happen to them.

A New York newspaper carried the story of a 38-year-old man who turned out to be the unluckiest man in his entire state. He was nearly electrocuted in a construction accident and was in a coma for a week. He recovered from that and was forced to hire a law firm to fight for his liability claims. One of his lawyers was disbarred, another died and his wife ran off with the other and filed for her divorce. Still his problems were not over.

He was stricken with a heart and liver disease that required him to be on oxygen continuously and he had to take 42 pills a day to survive.

Later he was involved in an auto accident. When the officers left someone came along and robbed him.

When the article was written, his benefits checks were cut off. His life's savings were depleted and his landlord had sent him an eviction notice. For some people, "If it weren't for bad luck, they would have no luck at all."

It seems that many of us live our lives by Murphy's Law that says, "If anything can go wrong, it will go wrong." My explanation is simply this –

That's How It Is Down Here.
If It's Not One Thing, It's Another.

In the city of Lystra, the Apostle Paul had been instrumental in the healing of a crippled man who had been lame from birth. Later, his enemies (self-righteous Jews) came to Lystra and incited a crowd to do Paul some bodily harm. People began to stone him. When they thought he was dead, they dragged him outside the city to the area where the dead were taken to be disposed. Believers then encircled Paul. Together they prayed for him,

Suddenly Paul was resuscitated and brought back to life. This was but one incident in this believer's life. Paul suffered much because of his belief and faith in Christ.

In the life of the Apostle Paul –
"If It's Not One Thing, It Was Another."
Five different times the Jews gave him thirty-nine lashes. Three times he was beaten with rods. Once he was stoned.

Three times he was shipwrecked. Once he testified that he was in the open sea all night and the next day.

Paul traveled many weary miles and he was often in danger from flooded rivers, from robbers, from his own people, the Jews as well as the Gentiles.

The Apostle Paul is, to many of us believers, the example of what every Christian should be like. But there are some things we sometimes tend to forget.

God allowed Paul a thorn in the flesh. Though Paul prayed to God three times to remove this, God refused, replying 'My grace is all you need.' Power comes to its full strength in weakness.

God allowed Paul to live with that thorn, that persistent perplexity, in order that Christ's power be perpetually evident in his life.

There are several things I want to say about this and I'm through.

First, I think you will agree with me when I say

PAUL LEARNED HOW TO LIVE WITH PERSISTENT PERPLEXITY.

For Paul, if it was not one thing it was another.

His was the perplexity f weakness. God allowed his perplexity of weakness to be his thorn in the flesh.

Biblical Scholars aren't in agreement as to what Paul's thorn was – it could have been physical, emotional, social, mental or spiritual. Whatever it was, God had a greater plan for him than the restoration of his health.

Paul also learned to live with the perplexity of rejection. He visited many towns where his own fellow Jews cast him out. It was because of the accusation of fellow Jews that Paul was kept in chains, destined for an early death.

Paul also knew the perplexity of persecution. His persecution caused him to be a very lonely man. Furthermore, Paul suffered the perplexity of hardship. He knew poverty. He knew pain, extreme misfortunes and extreme misery.

For Paul – **If it was not one thing, it was another.**

This brings me to the next thought.

SAINTS AND SINNERS IN THIS LIFE HAVE THEIR SHARE OF TROUBLES AND TRIALS.

We could say many of us learn, as Paul did, to live with persistent perplexity. Troubles and trials for us are as inevitable as a rainy day after you have washed and polished your car.

The Psalmist writes – **"Many are the afflictions of the righteous."**

The story is told of a boxer who was in the fight of his life. From the very first round he was being hit everywhere but under the bottom of his feet.

After the first round, he returned to his corner with his nose bleeding. But his manager, wanting to encourage him, so he said, "Good fight Champ. He never laid a glove on you."

After the second round, he returned to his corner with a bloody nose and a black eye. Again his manager wanting to encourage him, said to him, "Good fight Champ. He never laid a glove on you."

After the third round he practically crawled back to his corner. Now he has his nose bleeding and he has two black eyes. His manager's words were, "Good fight Champ. He never laid a glove on you."

The fighter took his mouthpiece out and said, "You say he never hit me. Do me a favor and keep your eye on that referee because somebody is beating the living daylights out of me."

Christians need to open their eyes because the devil is beating the stuffing out of us also.

You think you will never have troubles – stick around awhile and trouble, unsolicited and unsuspected, will come knocking at your door.

IF IT'S NOT ONE THING, IT'S ANOTHER.

By the time you get your car paid for, it's falling apart. If it's not the tires, it's the brakes. If it's not the transmission, the wheels need an alignment.

Get your car problems solved, the house gets into the act, the roof leaks. Get the roof replacement then discover that termites are eating away the foundation.

By the time you get your taxes paid, the insurance is due. If the furnace doesn't need fixing, the air conditioner needs to be replaced. If it's not the paint, it's the plumbing.

IF IT'S NOT ONE THING, IT'S ANOTHER.

Our bodies often trouble us. If it's not our eyesight, it's your hearing. If it's not your lungs, it's your kidneys. If your hair is not falling out, your teeth need fixing. If your back is not aching, your feet do. And if arthritis don't stop you from walking, laryngitis will stop you from talking.

IF IT'S NOT ONE THING, IT'S ANOTHER.

Saints and sinners alike learn how to live with persistent perplexity. This brings me to my final thought.

In spite of our persistent perplexities **WE CAN BE OVERCOMERS AND WE CAN BE VICTORIOUS!**

Many difficult problems loom like mountains, seeming too large to be solved. But say with the songwriter, "If I never had a problem, I'd never know that God would solve them."

We can be over-comers. We can be victorious.

Here's how it's done.

First, I think I need to tell us, we must never underestimate the power of God's promises.

God is almighty. He is the Creator of Heaven and earth. Like the Apostle Paul, we can take courage and say, "For I believe God. It will be just as He said."

As for me, I've seen the lightening flashing. I hear the thunder roar, etc. "He promised never to leave me alone."

Never underestimate the power of God's promise.

Also, as we are forced to live with persistent perplexity, believe that there is a purpose for every trial. Remember even in our trials, they are not about us, it's all about Him.

Think of God's intentions in allowing the trials to come our way. God may be allowing us an opportunity to prove ourselves, what we are made of, what our private actions are, what our personal lives are like.

Trials are always a test, a test of our wisdom, our faith, our integrity and our maturity. God allows trials to come to us to help, not hurt us. To make us, not break us, to strengthen us, not weaken us.

When we encounter trials it gives God the opportunity to reveal His grace, His love, His wisdom, His mercy as well as His blessings to us in special and sometimes spectacular ways.

While living with persistent perplexity, it would do well for us to believe that there is a purpose for every trial.

I've got to close this message –

I was discharged from the Marines in the Spring of 1946. I applied for enrollment at American Baptist College in the fall of that year. In the meanwhile, I had nothing to do. Someone told me to apply for unemployment and I was told I could receive $20.00 a week for 52 weeks just for being in the Service. I applied and received several checks.

In the meantime I helped my Sister with odd jobs around the house. One day I told her I was tired of doing nothing. So, I went and told the Counselor at the Employment Office, "Any kind of work, I'll do it." So at 4:00 that evening I was sent out near the airport to help open a restaurant for business.

We started around 5:00 p.m. and worked all night long washing dishes, scrubbing floors, stocking the pantry, putting meat in the freezer until daybreak.

The restaurant was to open at 8:00 that morning. A crew was to come in and open the restaurant. The crew did come in minus a dishwasher. Whereupon the man came to us looking to one of us to help him solve his problem.

I was the youngest person in the crowd. Everyone had an excuse – Doctor's appointments, sick relatives, need to be there to let wife go to work, physical inability, you name it. I stood there speechless, couldn't think of an excuse.

I said to one of those fellows, "All right looks like I'm the one. I'll stay until noon although I've been here like others all night long. But take this name and number, call my Sister. If I don't show up at home, she will be worried. Tell her for me 'I'll be home after a while. The man I'm working for has asked me to work here a little while long.'

I think of all my many minister friends, J. H. Dotson, J. C. Jackson, T. O. Chappelle, Sr., C. L. West, J. H. Johnson, M. D. Johnson, Norman Kerry, recently, my Pastor, Dr. H. Collier. Some better by nature than I have been by practice, punched their clocks and gone on home.

I'll be home after a while, the Man I'm working for has asked me to work on here a little while longer.

Lessons We Learned From Katrina

Many are the afflictions of the righteous,
but the Lord delivers him out of them all.
~ Psalm 34:19 ~
NKJV

People who do what is right have many
problems but the Lord solves them all
~ Psalm 34:19 ~
EDB

God, even our God, has navigated the circumstances of our lives and has brought us through the year 2005 into the third month of 2006. Time flies – I've learned that it flies only in one direction – it flies away from us.

As we move ahead into this New Year, it is my desire that all of our troubles be as short-lived as the New Year's Resolutions we made.

The year 2005 was quite a year. It could easily leave you feeling numb. The natural disasters during 2005 included Tsunami in the Pacific, the hurricanes on the Gulf Coast, flooding in the Northeast United States and Central America, the earthquakes in Central Asia, plus the wars in Iraq and Afghanistan.

There were terrorist attacks in London, Indonesia, Iraq, Russia and Israel. You would think we had seen enough. And then came Katrina. Along with other cities that were heavily hit, New Orleans seems to have been hit the worse.

There we saw a city sitting in 20 feet of water Citizens backing their way onto roofs of their dwellings, helicopters hovering over neighborhoods.

We further saw optimistic rescuers, opportunistic looters, grateful people and resentful people. We have seen it all.

Ask someone who's supposed to be in the know to solve the mystery for us, quietly and reverently they would probably tell us, "It is but one of the facts of life, "*That's How It Is Down Here. If It's Not One Thing, It's Another.*

In previous years I have said that troubles and trials are as sure as a rainy day after you have washed and polished your car. I have also said that troubles, trials, even tribulations are but one penalty belonging to the human race. We had no trouble before we were born and we will have none when we are gone. Jesus put it in the fine print of the believer's contract – "In this life ye shall have tribulations." *That's How It Is Down Here. If It's Not One Thing, It's Another.*

Even so, we have these encouraging words from the sacred scriptures, people who do what is right have many problems, but the Lord solves them all.

Tonight I want to talk from this all import subject – **THE LESSONS KATRINA TAUGHT US.**

Is God sending us a message? I think we would be wise if we paid attention. There are without a doubt some spiritual lessons God would want us to learn through this tragedy.

The first lesson is, **THE NATURE OF POSSESSIONS (TEMPORARY).**

As you listened to the evacuees and the survivors, we noticed their words. No one complained about the loss of plasma television set or a submerged SUV. No one was found running through the street yelling, "My cordless drill is missing, my golf clubs got washed away."

Their mourns were for people lost. If they rejoiced, it was for people found. Could Jesus be reminding us that people matter more than possessions?

In this land of ours where there are more malls than there are high schools, where there is more debt that credit, more clothes than we can ever wear, could Christ be saying to us, watch out! Beware of covetousness, for man's life doesn't consist in the abundance of his possessions.

We saw an entire riverboat casino washed up three blocks and placed on top of a house in a neighborhood. We saw demolished $40,000 cars submerged in 20 feet of water, never to be driven again.

Raging hurricanes and broken levees have a way of prying our fingers off the stuff we love. What was once precious can mean little, what we once ignored can immediately have eternal significance.

Through Katrina Christ tells us: stuff doesn't matter, people do. We learn from Katrina, the nature of possessions they are only temporary.

We also learn the nature of people (there are sinners and saints). To put it in the language of the street **THERE ARE SAINTS AND THE AINTS.**

We saw the most incredible servants and stories of selflessness and sacrifice. We saw people of the projects rescuing their neighbors, we saw civil servants risking their lives for people they had never seen before and perhaps would never see again.

A six year old girl tells about a helicopter man who picked her off the roof of a third story porch. He never sought any applause. She never got his name. All she know is, he saved her life. We saw humanity at its best. Likewise, we saw humanity at its worst.

We witnessed looting and fighting. We heard stories of rapes and robberies. Someone put it this way – just as the Heavens declared the glory of God, the streets were declaring the sinfulness of man.

We saw people of both dignity and depravity. The hurricane blew back more than roofs. It blew the masks off the human nature of mankind.

I think I need to tell us the main problem in our world is not Mother Nature, it's human nature. Strip away the police barricades, blow down the fences and the real self is revealed. We were born with a "me first" mentality.

Isaiah said, "All we like sheep have gone astray." Many have left God's path to follow their own. Left to our own devices, we lead a godless out of control life doing what we feel like doing when we feel like doing it.

What we learned from Katrina, the nature of people, Saints and sinners.

III. The third and final lesson we learn from Katrina – **THE NATURE OF GOD'S GRACE INSIDE AND OUT.**

God is great, and so great the heavens of Heaven cannot contain Him, yet He fills the entire universe with His presence.

All power belongs to Him. He speaks and it happens. He commands and it's done. Nothing is done but what He is totally and keenly aware of. This includes

Every wind that blows
Every bird that sings
Every flower that blooms
Every rain drop that falls
Every grain of sand that moves
Every wave that flows
Every activity that occurs.

He sees all, hears all, and knows all. His word is final. Nobody is above Him. He always was and He is still running this business.

If He did not exist, there would be no solutions to problems, no answers to questions, no victory to win, no reason to live, and no future to look forward to. He still hears and answers prayers.

Those who survived Katrina, some are still saying, "If it had not been for the Lord on my side, where would I be?"

This reminds me, a good Christian woman said to her minister following a terrible storm, "Pastor, during that storm I took shelter in a safe place, and I prayed that night like I'd never prayed before. My life was spared but the roof blew off my house. It even moved some from its foundation. How can you say, God answers prayers?"

The minister calmly said, "Sister, you said you prayed like you never prayed before? Her response, "That's correct." His reply was, "Maybe God was off taking care of His regular customers."

From Katrina we learn the nature of things temporary; the nature of Saints and sinners, and the nature of God – grace inside and out.

When we are down, three lessons we learn:

Those we thought would help, won't
Those you thought wouldn't, will
The most important lesson is God will send some help your way. When the Lord says, "Yes," it's done.

I close with this:

It is not what you accomplish that makes the difference. It's not what you possess. But it is what you are.

Love – real genuine – God-given love – Christ-like – heartfelt generous love will do something to you, for you and through you that nothing else can.

A friend of mine of the yesteryears tells of his car breaking down on a seldom traveled road at least ten miles from the nearest town.

What do you do when you don't know what to do? He prayed, he waited, and he prayed some more. When he was about to lose hope he observed a car coming at a distance. The man was kind enough to stop. Seeing he was in need of help, he got out, tried to get the man's car running again. When he failed to get the car started, he opened the trunk of his car, took out a tow chain, hooked it on to his car and towed him to the nearest garage in the closest town.

Told him to wait until morning, a mechanic there would fix his car. The man was so grateful he offered to pay him whatever his charges were for towing him into the city.

When he persisted in paying him, he asked him one question, "Sir, do you have a tow chain in the trunk of your car?" His response was, "I'm sorry, I do not." He then said, "Then while the mechanic is repairing your car, stop by the local hardware store, pick up a tow chain, put it in your car."

Why would I do that?"

"If no other reason to make it up to me." As you travel over the highway of life, the blessing that has come to you, pass it on to someone else. By so doing, you will be following in the footprints of Jesus.

Jesus went on to Calvary to save our souls from the torments of Hell. We need to spend our days making it up to Him.

What Can We Do When Trouble Comes?

"Many are the afflictions of the righteous, but the Lord delivers him out of them all.
~Psalm 34.19 ~
(NKJV)

"I will lift up my eyes to the hills from whence comes my help."
~ Psalm 121:1 ~
(NKJV)

Have you ever had bad days when you simply could not win? One fellow was driving home from work one evening and heard a radio announcer suggest to his listeners that they surprise their mates when they got home. "When you arrive for dinner," he said, "instead of growling something like, 'when will dinner be ready?' why not surprise your wife with a little gift?"

The man thought that sounded like a good idea, so he stopped along the way for a bouquet of flowers and a box of candy. Instead of driving into the garage, he went up to the front door and rang the bell.

His wife opened the door, saw him standing there with a radiant smile on his face, holding out his gifts to her. But she declared crankily to him, "Well, if this don't beat it all? Listen Buster, the baby has colic, the washing machine is broken again, and Junior got into a fight at school today and got expelled. Now you make my day perfect by coming home drunk!"

Trouble, no one likes it, but no one is very successful in avoiding it. In one way or another trouble seems to be a fact of life. Trouble has no age preference. It invades the life of a young person as well as the old.

Trouble has no respect for gender, race or social circle. Trouble invades the life of the rich and the famous. Trouble also visits the unknown and the poor.

Trouble, one product in which the supply exceeds the demand. Trouble is as inevitable as a rainy day after you have washed and polished your car. It is also a penalty we all must pay, because we all belong to the human race.

That's how it is down here –

IF IT'S NOT ONE THING, IT'S ANOTHER.

Tonight I want to attempt to answer a very important question – **WHAT CAN WE DO WHEN TROUBLE COMES?**

"Grit your teeth and bear it" is the philosophy many would suggest when trouble comes. For trivial matters, especially troubles of our own making, this might work.

If you have lived as long as I have, you realize that there is good trouble and bad trouble. But my message tonight is to realize that a dark shadow can fall across the path in your life or mine that God can't shine His light upon.

The Psalmist tells us we can give our problems to God. He says, "I will lift up mine eyes to the hills from whence comes my help; my help comes from the Lord who made the heaven and earth."

My first thought is this – **IF YOU FIND A PATH THAT HAS NO TROUBLE, YOU WILL ALSO FIND THAT IT LEADS TO NOWHERE.**

Paul Harvey once said, 'you can always tell when you are on the road to success, it is up-hill all the way.'

Trouble, like crosses, comes in all sizes. As soon as you get your car paid for, it's falling apart. If it's not the tires, it's the brakes. If it's not the transmission, it's the wheels that need an alignment.

Get your car troubles solved, house problems begin. The roof leaks. Get the roof replaced then you discover the termites are eating away the foundation. By the time the taxes are paid, the insurance becomes due.

If it's not the furnace that needs fixing, it's the compressor in the air conditioning unit that needs to be replaced. If it's not the paint, it's the plumbing.

IF IT'S NOT ONE THING, IT'S ANOTHER.

Our bodies cause us trouble. They may appear to be as beautiful as the starry skies, but they are as fading as a summer flower. If it's not your lungs, it's your kidneys. If your hair is not falling out, your teeth need fixing. If your back is not hurting, your feet are giving you trouble.

And if arthritis doesn't stop you from walking, laryngitis will stop you from talking. If you don't have a cold, you are burning up with fever.

If it's not one thing, it's another.

As for life at church, if it's not the program, it's the budget. Get the Auxiliaries functioning properly, trouble is found somewhere else. When the shepherd is forced to speak well of the wolf, the sheep are in serious trouble.

If nobody knows the troubles you've seen, you don't live in a small town. If, in this life, you find a path that has no trouble, you will also find that it leads to nowhere.

That's how it is down here.
If it's not one thing, It's another.

So much for trouble. The question I planned to answer during the second half of this message tonight is – **WHAT CAN WE DO WHEN TROUBLE COMES?**

II. Here are four suggestions to allow God's help to reach us.

First, I would suggest that we TRY TO VIEW TROUBLE OBJECTIVELY.

Establishing a proper perspective is indeed a difficult task. It is important that you would ask some questions of yourself.

Most of the trouble is of the minor nature we have brought on ourselves. God has equipped us with a sense of humor. We ought to use it to take a good look at ourselves.

It takes two things to blow down a tree. A heavy wind outside and rot and decay inside. So it is with man. The winds of adversity may cause him to bend, but if he is strong and vigorous within, he will arise and grow to new heights after the storm passes.

He knows not his own strength who has not met with adversity. To answer the question, **what to do when trouble comes**, first, try to view the trouble objectively.

Secondly, when troubles come, **WE MUST SEE THEM AS GOD'S OPPORTUNITIES.** We must not wallow in self-pity asking why did this have to happen to me.

We ought not to bristle in resentment, nor brood over our troubles. We ought not fret or complain. Trouble will make you and me bitter or better. Our God is a sovereign God. He overrules all things for the ultimate good of those who love Him.

The gem cannot be polished without friction nor the child of God cleansed without adversity.

Here's a parable of the over-comer. The parable is told of an old dog that fell in the farmer's well. After assessing the situation, the farmer sympathized with the dog and decided that neither the dog nor the well was worth saving.

He decided to bury the dog and put him out of his misery. The farmer began shoveling dirt into the well. The dog was hysterical. As the farmer began shoveling dirt on his back, he would shake it off and step up. He kept shaking it off and stepping up, and at last could step out of the well.

No matter how painful the blow or how distressing the situation, remember the problem designed to bury us can benefit us if we shake them off and step out of the well we find ourselves in. When trouble comes, see them as opportunities.

Here's another thought. <u>WHEN TROUBLE COMES, REMEMBER GOD TAKES US THROUGH A MULTITUDE OF EXPERIENCES THAT WERE NOT MEANT FOR US AT ALL;</u> they are meant to make us more useful in His hands., God sometimes bring us through it to get us to it.

Troubles not only develop character, they reveal it. Also when trouble comes, **WE MUST LOOK OUTSIDE OURSELVES TO THE SOURCE OF ALL OUR STRENGTH.**

When the Psalmist asks, 'from whence cometh my help?' his answer is, 'my help comes from the Lord." There are three ways God's help comes to us.

First, it is by **PRAYER.** Man is never as tall as when he kneels before God, never as great as when he humbles himself before God. And the man who kneels to God can stand up to anything.

Dr. Jesse Jai McNeil's Mother, who told her son on her sick bed dying of cancer, when asked, are you praying? Her answer was, "I am not. A long time ago when the blood flowed warm in my veins, I prayed then, now I can trust."

I've found that the greatest power in this world is the power of prayer.

Another way God helps us is by **BIBLE STUDY.** Growth in grace and in knowledge of the Lord can be obtained only through in-depth Bible Study.

These words of caution when trouble comes – "Keep traveling this road. When you reach and cross that river, your road is going to change."

Here Comes Trouble Again

"Before I was afflicted I went astray,
but now I have kept your words."
~ Psalm 119:67 ~
(NKJV)

"It is good for me that I have been
afflicted that I may learn your statues."
~ Psalm 119:71 ~
(NKJV)

There are many things a congregation of this size will disagree on, but one thing we all would agree on is we live in a world that has a lot of trouble.

Life can do some terrible things to us. It can rob us of our health, our friends, and our possessions. It can crush us, and leave us beaten and broken.

Our nation is in trouble when it comes to our families. Our morals, our government, our schools, even when it comes to our churches, everybody that you and I know has had or will have some kind of trouble.

The trouble may be mental or emotional, financial or even materialistic, the trouble may be physical or even spiritual. Everybody has something, some situation in their life which can well be classified as trouble.

For the past thirty years, I have stood behind this sacred desk and told you what I know about trouble. I have used the subject, **'If It's Not One Thing, It's Another."** Tonight with the help with the Divine Spirit I hope not to give you the same soup warmed over. I thought to use this very simple subject, which is, **"HERE COMES TROUBLE."**

The Psalmist says, 'before I was afflicted I went astray, but now I have kept your words.' (Psalm 119:67)

'It was good for me that I have been afflicted, that I learn your statues.' (Psalm 119:71)

Three practical things I want to say about trouble.

First, I want to say a word about who's causing trouble.

Second, I would like to share with you what I believe are the benefits and blessings of trouble.

And last but not least, I would dare to tell us how to handle trouble when it comes.

WHO IS THE CAUSE OF OUR TROUBLE?

When a person finds his or herself in a world of trouble, they generally look for someone to blame them on. Can I tell us that many of the problems and troubles we have we bring on ourselves? Sometimes we even blame them on God.

When we were growing up as a child, we were told that those bodies of ours needed good nutrition, good rest, and good exercise. We deprived these bodies of these things and when we start having health problems, we cannot understand how the good Lord of Heaven can allow those terrible things to happen to us.

King David had a lot of problems and he brought most of them on himself. Generally when people begin to recognize that they brought the problems on themselves, there is some hope for them. No one goes around looking for trouble. It seems that trouble is always looking for us.

This brings me to my next thought – **THE BENEFITS OR THE BLESSINGS OF TROUBLE.**

Trouble can be man's best friend. Trouble comes to make us strong. We admire strong people all across the nation. There are weight lifting contests where men compete to see who is the strongest.

A life of ease will destroy a Christian. The untroubled life is often a shallow life. Many of us will never rise to our full potential without going through some tough times.

Can I tell you, **Here Comes Trouble Again** to make us strong? Trouble also comes to make us sympathetic. It takes suffering to make one understand suffering. It takes heartaches to understand heartaches. It takes loneliness to understand loneliness. It takes poverty to understand poverty.

One of the big mistakes we make in this country, we keep sending rich people to Washington, D. C. that know very little about the suffering of the average citizen.

Unless you have been in need, it is difficult to understand a person in need. Here comes trouble to make us more sympathetic.

Here comes trouble again, also to make us more spiritual. David confesses, 'before I was afflicted, I went astray, but now I have kept your word.'

46

Any experience we have that brings us closer to God is always a blessing. So, trouble comes to make us strong, trouble comes to make us sympathetic, trouble comes to make us more spiritual.

Nothing short of disaster or some other calamity will cause many to become aware of God and their desperate need of Him. One lady told her pastor that during the tornado that destroyed her home, 'Pastor I prayed like I had never prayed before that my house would be spared. Tell me what happened. My house was almost totally destroyed. Pastor explain to me why God didn't answer my Prayer?'

The pastor's comment was, 'you said you prayed like you had never prayed before. Maybe God was busy taking care of His regular customers.'

Here comes trouble again – to make us strong, to make us sympathetic and to make us spiritual.

This brings me to the final part of this message.

Some ideas, some rules for handling trouble when it comes – **TWO WAYS OF FACING TROUBLE.**

When trouble comes, the Psalmist suggests two ways of dealing with trouble, two ways to try to meet it.

One way is to try to run away from it and the other way is to face it with God's help. The Psalmist said, 'Oh that I had wings like a dove, then would I fly away and be at rest.' (Psalm 5:22)

Jonah tried this fly away philosophy. God told him to preach in Nineveh. Jonah didn't like the people in Nineveh, so he decided to run away.

He went down to Joppa and bought a ticket to Tallish which was in the opposite direction. But Jonah never reached that destination. He paid for a ticket but he couldn't ride.

Jonah wanted a place where there were no problems but found out there is no such place on this earth.

Instead of avoiding trouble, Jonah invited it, as people generally do when they try to run away from themselves and their responsibilities. When Jonah chose the way of obedience the Lord sustained him in ways he had not dreamed of.

The Psalmist also gave us another way to deal with trouble. He writes, 'cast thy burdens on the Lord and He will sustain thee.' (Psalm 55:22)

I found this out about our Lord. Every load He places on our shoulders He places His own arm underneath to help us to bear them.

To cast thy burden upon the Lord is the religious person's answer to his troubles. For experience reveals that when we are faithful, even though we may suffer, God is able to sustain us in ways we had not realized until we put our trust in Him.

I'm going to close this message by saying it is possible to be headed in the right direction but on the wrong road. I had the experience of traveling several miles in the right direction but on the wrong road.

Instead of going back, I decided to take a short cut to the right road. The short cut was rough and rocky, with washed out places in the road.

Made an inquiry – is this the road that will put me on the right road, etc. Farmer told me to keep traveling this road. After a while you will cross a river and the road is going to change…

Good People Have Troubles Too

*"Many are the afflictions of the righteous,
but the Lord delivereth him out of them all."*
~ Psalm 34:19 ~
(NKJV)

*"The good man does not escape all troubles,
he has them too. But the Lord helps him in
each and every one."*
(Living Bible Paraphrase)

What would life be without trouble or a trial? Neither you nor I will ever know, because troubles and trials are as inevitable as a rainy day after you have washed your car and, they appear to be the penalties for our belonging to the human race.

There are some people who have the notion or who seem to believe that Christians are, or ought to be, exempt from trials and troubles. However, this notion cannot be proven by any reader of God's Holy Word.

The Bible teaches this, and experience teaches the same thing, that as hard as you try and as good as you try to be, trouble, unsolicited and unexpected, comes to us all.

The Psalmist has declared that, "Many are the afflictions of the righteous, but the Lord delivereth him out of them all."

The Living Bible quotes the Psalmist saying, even, "The good man does not escape all troubles, he has them too. But the Lord helps him in each and every one."

My message today tells us, **IF IT'S NOT ONE THING, IT'S ANOTHER.** Let me explain my subject by sharing a personal experience.

I have one automobile that I have been driving eleven years. I have kept it so long that it is now worth more to me than it would be to anyone else.

A few weeks ago trouble developed in the transmission. I got that fixed then the brakes failed. I got them adjusted then I woke up one morning with a flat tire. I bought a new set of tires and on that same day I walked out in a hurry to meet a couple to perform a marriage, and it wouldn't start, which resulted in the purchase of a new battery.

At first I thought I had been picked out to be picked on, but then it came to me like the peal of a bell on a clear night. That's how it is down here, you need to tell others about it. **IF IT'S NOT ONE THING, IT'S ANOTHER.**

CHRISTIANS HAVE TROUBLES TOO

The first point I want to make is this – Christians have troubles too. Even for Christians, **if it's not one thing, it's another.**

Here's a respected Christian leader who wakes up one morning to hear his wife of 25 years tell him she wants a divorce so that she can live her own life; or a faithful Christian wife who is dumbfounded when her Christian husband tells her that he feels led by the Lord to leave her to marry someone else.

There is that God-fearing doctor who receives a call from the police saying they are holding his son who is charged with selling drugs.

Then there's that Godly farm couple who weeps as their unwed daughter tells them she is to have a child. **If it's not one thing, it's another.**

The recent flood of our city sent water, like a swollen river, through certain sections of the city; and, it was not just worldly folk, but a lot of law abiding, Christian people who lost all they had. Good people have trouble too.

There was Job who is a living witness to the fact that **if it's not one thing, it's another.** He was a righteous successful agriculturist, yet he lost all of his earthly possessions. His was a close knit family. All of his children were killed in a storm at the same time. Before he could recover from this tragedy, sores broke out all over his body, and as if this was not enough, his wife irritates and worries him.

Good people have troubles too. **If it's not one thing, it's another.**

WE ARE CONFRONTED WITH PROBLEMS

In life's great school of experience, we learn that in this life we are confronted with problem after problem. And these problems, like crosses, come in many sizes.

It could be a flat tire on a freeway when you are already late for an urgent appointment; or, like running out of gas on a lonely road in a strange unfamiliar country side. **If it's not one thing, it's another.**

It's like remembering today an appointment you forgot yesterday; or it's a personal injury accident in which you are at fault, and to your surprise your liability insurance policy premium was not paid; or it is the mortgage payment which is past due, and you are without a job and no funds left in the savings account.

In this life we are confronted with problem after problem. **If it's not one thing, it's another.**

As soon as one problem is solved there are two to take its place. By the time the car is paid for, you need a new motor. If it is not a set of tires, the brakes need replacing. If it's not the transmission, the wheels need alignment.

When you get the car problem solved, it's the house – the roof leaks. When the roof is repaired, you discover termites are eating the supports of the foundation. By the time the taxes are paid, the insurance becomes due.

If it is not the heating unit which needs fixing, it's the air conditioner. If it's not the paint, it's the plumbing. **If it's not one thing, it's another.**

Even the elements of nature get in on the act. If it is not too hot, it's too cold; if it is not snowing, it's raining; if it's not a tornado watch, it's a severe storm or a flash flood watch. **If it's not one thing, it's another.**

Even our physical bodies get in on the action. These bodies of ours may be as beautiful as the starry sky, but they are as fading as a summer flower. If it's not your eyesight, it's your hearing. If it's not your lungs, it's your kidneys. If it's not your hair falling out, it's your teeth that need fixing.

If it's not your back that is hurting, it's our feet that are giving you trouble. If it's not too much weight, it's not enough weight. If it's not arthritis that stops you from walking, it's laryngitis that stops you from talking.

If you don't have a cold, you are burning up with a fever. **If it's not one thing, it's another.**

LIVE LIFE FROM DAY TO DAY

Having faced up to this fact, **IF IT'S NOT ONE THING, IT'S ANOTHER**, how then are we to live life at its fullest from day to day? May I offer a few suggestions which might help?

Every day of your life, make that extra effort to stand on the promises of God. The text here says, "The good man does not escape all troubles, he has them too. But the Lord helps him in each and every one."

Whatever the trouble is, there is a point of advantage for the child of God. He has the assurance that in his troubles, he is not alone. With Christ on your side, you are bound to win.

Another way to make it is through determination. In this life you are bound to have some defeats, but make up your mind not to allow your defeats to defeat you. My dad put it like this, "It's not the size of the dog in the fight, it's the size of the fight in the dog that wins the battle."

Then remember, trouble don't last always. The Lord delivers us out of them all. Remember, weeping may endure for the night, but joy cometh in the morning. You can't hold back the dawn. The song writer puts it like this:

Oh, Lord, you know, all about my troubles;
Oh, Lord, you know, all about my trials and tribulations;
It ain't been easy, traveling this road in your name,
But I trust you Lord, do the work in my life;
Oh I trust you Lord, do the work in my life.
Use my hands, my feet, yes Lord – yes Lord
Use my hands, my feet, yes Lord – yes Lord
It ain't been easy, traveling this road in your name,
But I trust you Lord, do the work in my life;
Oh I trust you Lord, do the work in my life.

I close with this –

Some years ago, one of our members had a daughter in an Oklahoma City hospital, and it was reported that she was not going to recover.

Since she grew up here in our church, I felt it necessary to go there and pray with and for her. It seemed that I would never find the time, but one morning I decided to make time, and without telling anyone I took off for Oklahoma City. I had gotten about midway of the turnpike when I felt and heard a tire going flat. All along that turnpike there are those emergency telephones about ten miles apart. The Lord was truly with me. When I brought my car to a stop, I was exactly in front of the emergency phone.

Although I had a spare, I was dressed for a hospital visit, and I really didn't know too much about changing a flat tire. Therefore, I picked up the phone and proceeded to tell the man who answered where I was. The man said, "I know where you are, just tell me what you need."

Let me tell you something about the Lord. We have a royal telephone in our bosoms. We can call Him anytime day or night. We don't have to tell where we are, or even what the problem is, just tell Him what we want.

Our God is a "flat tire" fixer. He has fixed many flat tires for me. Even when I have a flat tire with Him, I am still encouraged because, as with all flat tires, they are flat on but one side. With His help, I'm on the go again.

Jesus knows all about our struggles,
He will guide till the day is done;
There's not a friend like the lowly Jesus
No, not one! No, not one!

How To Handle Trouble

"Many are the afflictions of the righteous
but the Lord delivers him out of them all."
~ Psalm 34:19 ~
(NKJV)

Permit me to introduce this sermon tonight by telling you a true story I learned about Chippie, the parakeet.

Chippie never saw it coming. One second he was peacefully perched in his cage sending a glad song into the air. The next second he was sucked into the line of the vacuum cleaner.

His problem began when his owner decided to clean his cage with a vacuum sweeper. She stuck the nozzle in the cage to suck up the feathers and seeds at the bottom when the nearby phone rang.

She had barely said hello when swoooppp, Chippie was sucked in. Quickly she let the phone drop, switched off the vacuum. With her heart in her mouth, she quickly unzipped the bag. There was Chippie stunned but alive.

He was covered with heavy gray dust. She then grabbed him up, rushed him to the bathroom, turned on the faucet full blast and held Chippie under the torrent of cold water, power washing him clean.

Then it dawned on her that Chippie was soaking wet and shivering cold. Whereupon, she did what any compassionate pet owner would do, she snatched up her hair dryer and blasted him with hot air.

The question is, did Chippie survive? Yes, he did! But he doesn't sing much anymore. He just sits and stares a lot, as if wondering as to what other new experience may be forth coming.

You can almost understand why. Within ten minutes and a few seconds, Chippie had been sucked in, washed up and blown over. It's enough to steal the song from any stout heart.

I told Chippie's story to make one point – all the bad unenlisted, unexpected things that happened to Chippie can and could very well happen to any one of us. And that's what this sermon is about tonight, **"That's How It Is Down Here, If It's Not One Thing It Is Another."**

The Psalmist made this observation, "Many are the afflictions of the righteous but the Lord delivers him out of them all."

There are five things I want to say about this subject, **"How to Handle Trouble."**

> First I'm going to tell us – Expect trouble
> Refuse Satan an entrance into the door of your trouble
> Face trouble with prayer
> Reach out to others in trouble
> Refuse to look at trouble in the present tense.
> First I should tell us to **EXPECT TROUBLE**

Trouble and trials are as inevitable as a rainy day after you have washed and polished your car.

Trouble and trials are one of the penalties we all must pay just for belonging to the human race.

The text reads, "Many are the afflictions of the righteous…"

We live in a world where there is a potential for both good and evil. Jesus sent His disciples out as sheep in the midst of wolves because He knew the way of the cross would bring trouble. Trouble is inherent in life and we ought to live with that realistic attitude. These are terrible times in which we live.

These are times when –

Hypocrisy is extremely popular
Appearances are often deceiving
Integrity is proudly disregarded
Immorality is openly displayed in public places

These are indeed difficult times we live.

When we get a problem solved, a dozen more crop up

Just when things begin to run halfway smoothly, somebody throws a wrench on the works

Just when you think your bills are all paid up, some unexpected expense occurs

Just when you think you can handle the load you are carrying, something else gets piled on the load

And just when you think you're about to get your head above the water, something or someone pulls you back down again.

IF IT'S NOT ONE THING, IT'S ANOTHER

You may think you will never have any real trouble, but if you stay around long enough, trouble will come knocking at your door.

IF IT'S NOT ONE THING, IT'S ANOTHER

By the time you get your car paid for, it's falling apart. If it's not the tires, it's the brakes. If it's not the transmission, the wheels need alignment.

Get your car troubles solved, the house gets into the act, the roof leaks. Get the roof replaced, then you discover termites eating away the foundation.

By the time the taxes are paid, the insurance becomes due. Get the furnace fixed and the air conditioner unit also needs to be replaced. If it's not the paint, it's the plumbing.

IF IT'S NOT ONE THING, IT'S ANOTHER <u>EXPECT TROUBLE</u>

I challenge us next to **<u>REFUSE SATAN AN ENTRANCE THROUGH YOUR DOOR OF TROUBLE.</u>**

Our adversary will use trouble to make us bitter and angry towards God and cause us to withdraw from others.

You have to give much praise and respect to Job.

Job lost his property, his family, even his health. His respect among his friends, even his wife. Yet he refused to allow Satan an entrance through the door of his trouble.

You hear him saying, "The Lord gave and the Lord has taken away – etc."

"Though He slay me, yet will I trust Him – etc."

"I know my redeemer liveth – etc."

Jesus said to Peter as he faced the troubling hours of the cross, "Simon, Simon, Satan desires to have you that he might sift you as wheat, but I prayed for you that your faith fail not. When you are converted, strengthen the brethren."

Expect trouble, but don't let Satan have an entrance through the door of trouble.

Here's another suggestion on how to handle trouble.

FACE TROUBLE WITH PRAYER

The only way trouble should get us down is down on our knees in prayer. If we maintain through prayer, our fellowship with the Lord, we will experience the promise of the Psalmist, "Call upon me in the day of trouble. I will deliver you, and you shall glorify me." (Psalm 50:15)

In our troubles tell the Lord, "We need Him down here because sin has broken loose."

It's jumped into the water; it's shaken up the seas; it's climbed the mountains and kicked down the trees.

Tell God we need Him down here because mankind has not been kind at all. We're dying for reasons that remain untold. Sickness and diseases still unfold. Death is lurking with needles and dope. Claiming young lives and leaving no hope.

Old folk are going hungry, eating food from garbage cans, living in the streets with one pot and one pan. They're scared to walk the streets at night. They lock their doors, they tremble in fright.

We press our way to work to make ends meet. Come home to find our own sisters are being raped in the streets.

One way to handle trouble, we have to **face our troubles with prayer.**

I have another suggestion. **<u>REACH OUT TO OTHERS IN TROUBLE</u>**

Our own troubles become smaller when we reach out to others in love. God has a greater blessing for those who, in trouble themselves, will reach out to help another in trouble.

The widow of Zarephath is a good example. She attempted to feed the Prophet Elijah when she was living from the bottom of her barrel.

When she looked again, the Bible says as long as the famine was in the land, her meal barrel was never empty and her cruse of oil never failed.

It has been my own experience, when I've helped to dig someone out of their troubles, I've been able to leave a hole to bury my own. **Reach out to others in trouble.**

Finally, in handling trouble, **<u>REFUSE TO LOOK AT TROUBLE IN THE PRESENT TENSE.</u>**

Always look to the future and realize that God could be just bringing us through it to get us to it.

Our fore parents taught us, "trouble don't last always." Even the sun has a sinking spell every night. But it wakes up and goes about its round the next day.

God shapes us down here so that we can fit in up there.

There was a small child on a long journey west by train. Everyone on board was complaining. The child with no care in the world was asked why she was so happy. Her rely was, "It has truly been a tiresome journey, but I'm so happy. My Father's going to meet me at my journey's end."

Keep Me Till I Get Home

When The Worse Things Happen To The Best People

> *"Shall we indeed accept good from God*
> *and shall we not accept adversity?"*
> *~ John 10 ~*
> *(NKJV)*

Trouble, Trouble, Trouble – that may be what you're having in your life today. Thousands of people are having it rough in the times we are living in.

You may have so many problems with inflation, recession, unemployment, increasing bills and other needs that you feel like your middle name is trouble.

Even if we are faithful Christians and concerned human beings, we are trying our best to do right and to help others to do the same, this will not keep the troubles, trials and the storms of life from coming to any of us. Most of us have lived long enough to know that the worse things can happen to the best people.

For instance –

A young mother learns she has terminal cancer

A bus taking a church group to a ski-resort overturns injuring many and leaving a young mother paralyzed

A child crossing the street is struck by a drunken driver and is killed

A young father working a second job as a convenient store clerk is killed by a teenager on drugs who held up the store.

True stories like these fill our daily newspapers, they pervade our coffee time conversations, and they are the substance of countless prayer requests. All around us good people are hurting with anguish and tears.

And we find ourselves looking heavenward asking one over-riding question – WHY? Of all people, why her? Why him? Why me? Why us? The answer never comes easy.

Complex questions never have simple answers.

My father used to tell me when I was a child, and I hurled some complex problems to him, "It's only life, my child!

That's How It Is Down Here. If It's Not One Thing, It's Another."

There are three things I want to say about this and I'm through.

First I think I should tell us **MANY FOLK ARE ASKING HOW COULD A GOOD GOD MAKE A WORLD LIKE THIS WHERE SO MUCH OF THE**

SUFFERING FALLS ON THOSE WHO LEAST DESERVE IT?

We have the good example of the Old Testament man Job, one who went through extreme personal agony. The Book of Job is a real drama that begins like a fairy tale.

He is one of the wealthiest and most respected men in the East. He is surrounded by what are commonly regarded as unmistakable tokens of Divine favor. A large family, immense wealth, herds of cattle, sheep and camels, vigorous health, a good reputation and great power. It looked as though every cloud in Job's sky had a silver lining.

But before his story progresses very far, the dark clouds of sorrow and suffering gather over Job's pleasant life. Before the storm is over Job loses everything he values except his life and his faith.

As tragedy keeps striking the silver lining of Job's life, it turns to brass and he is almost plunged into the depths of despair. Job's wife and his friends add to his misery by offering cheap, easy answers to agonizing questions. Though they mean well, they do great harm. No one except God knows the quality of Job's faith until it is tested.

Satan tests Job. First of all his wealth is either stolen or destroyed by natural calamities. Then the house where all of his children have gathered is struck by a tornado and all ten of them die a violent death. Job remains true to God. His faith stands up to Satan's tests.

Satan never gives up easily on good people. The devil then proceeds to afflict Job's character. God gives him permission to afflict his body, but not to take his life.

His body is then covered with sores that cause excruciating pain and he is found sitting in the soft ashes of the city dump.

What a pathetic scene. Job, one of the greatest men of the East is now grieving and is destitute. His wealth is gone, his children are dead, and his body is wrecked with pain.

If that's not enough, his wife tells him that God doesn't play fair. She poses a simple solution – 'curse God and die.'

Job is wiser than his wife. He repeats the words of our text, "Shall we indeed accept the good from God and shall we not accept the bad?" Many folk are asking, like Job's wife, 'How could a good God make a world like this where so much suffering falls on those who least deserve it?' But, **THAT'S HOW IT IS DOWN HERE. IF IT'S NOT ONE THING, IT'S ANOTHER.**

TROUBLE, TROUBLE, AND TROUBLE –

THAT MAY BE WHAT YOU ARE HAVING IN YOUR LIFE TODAY.

Troubles, trials and tribulations are found in the believer's contract, we had no trouble before we were born, we will have none when we are gone. In this life you will have tribulations. **"IF IT'S NOT ONE THING, IT'S ANOTHER.**

By the time you get your car paid for, it's falling apart. If it's not the tires, it's the brakes. If it's not the transmission, it's the emission. Get our car problems solved, trouble develops at the home and the roof leaks. Get the roof repaired and discover termites are eating away the foundation.

Get your taxes paid, the insurance is due. If it's not the furnace, it's the air conditioner that needs to be replaced. If it's not the paint, it's the plumbing. **"IF IT'S NOT ONE THING, IT'S ANOTHER."**

Our bodies get in the act, especially folk above fifty. If it's not your eyesight, it's your hearing. If it's not your lungs, it's your kidneys. If it's not your hair that's falling out, your teeth need fixing. If arthritis don't stop you from walking, laryngitis will stop you from talking. **"IF IT'S NOT ONE THING, IT'S ANOTHER."**

My third and final thought is this – **<u>GOD DOES NOT SAVE US FROM TROUBLE, HE SAVES US IN TROUBLE.</u>**

We cannot always see how God works but He is always in the plan in the simplest ways.

Consider the little rabbit that was fascinated by his new found speed. The little bunny loves to outrun all the creatures of the woods. He outran the toad frog, and the snake. Nothing could ever catch him. In fact, he took on every creature of the forest to test his skills. The little rabbit was disturbed because each time his folk let him go to the woods alone, Mama Rabbit would prick the bottom of his foot with a thorn.

When they left him without an explanation, the rabbit limped around for hours in pain. After a while, concerned the little rabbit asked Mama Rabbit the question. Why do you prick my foot every time you leave me alone? It doesn't make any sense and it seems cruel for you to do me this way.

Mama Rabbit hopped over to her son and said,

"There's a hound dog and a hunter out there and they love to chase fast rabbits."

"Knowing you would give them a run, it may not make sense to you now, but it's better for you to be a living bunny with a sore foot, than a dead rabbit with a fast reputation."

It didn't make sense to him then, but his sore foot was keeping him alive.

God knows what's best for us. There is an unseen hand that guides and controls that tears down and builds us up. He does not save us from trouble. He saves us in trouble.

Trouble is not a gate crasher in the arena of our lives, it has a reserved seat, and the heartache has a pass key to every home in our land. Life is like a grindstone whether we are ground down or polished depends on what we are made of.

We seldom have control over what happens to us, but it's what happens in us that ultimately matters. I've lived a long time. Let me tell you seven things I've found –

I've found myself laughing at difficulties and have found them disappearing.

I've found myself attempting heavy responsibilities and found them growing lighter.

I've found myself facing bad situations and found it clearing up.

I've found myself telling the truth and found it to be the easiest way.

I've found myself doing an honest day's work and found it most rewarding.

I've found myself believing men honest and found many living up to my expectation.

I've found myself trusting God each day and found Him surprising me with His goodness.

Close with the illustration

I want to close this message by telling you about the experience that was mine following my discharge from the U. S. Marines.

I was told that I could receive unemployment compensation of $20.00 weekly for 52 weeks. I applied and received a check every other week for about four weeks.

In the meanwhile I did chores for my Sister around her house. When I ran out of work there, I went to the employment office and asked for a job, any job, I was tired of doing nothing. Besides, my father had said, "One's bread is sweeter if you work for it."

I took a job for $27.00 a week at a restaurant near the airport. I could have stayed at home and received $20.00 for doing nothing.

The first day I was on the job, I went to work around 5:00 p.m. and worked all night long, helping to open a restaurant for business at 8:00 a.m. the next day.

We worked hard. We scrubbed floors, washed dishes, set up tables, we did it all. We were to go home when our work of preparation was completed.

When it was time for us to go, the owner came where we were and said, "Fellows, I want to thank you for your good help last night. I know you're tired and need rest, but I've got a problem. I need someone to run the dishwasher this morning. The employment office will have someone here by noon. Who will it be?" All of the fellows were older than me. Each one had an excuse – dental appointment, children to drive to school, medication to take at a given hour. So I stood there without an excuse to give. Whereupon I said, "Fellows, I'm tired and weary even as you are. But it looks like I'm the one to do it. But do me a favor, take this number, call my sister when you get home. Tell her I'll be on home after a while. The man I'm working for wants me to work here a little while longer."

I think of my many friends who have punched their clocks and gone on home. I'll be on after a while. The man I'm working for wants me to work here a little while longer.

When the Saints Go Marching In, etc.

Where To Go, What To Do And Where To Look When Trouble Comes

"Many are the afflictions of the righteous, but the Lord delivereth him out of them all."
~ Psalm 34:19 ~
(NKJV)

It would be so nice if we could plan our lives and have everything according to those plans. But no matter how much we would want life to be like that, it is just not the way life is.

Job was a man who knew a lot about life and we find that he said after many pressures and perplexing problems, 'man that is born of a woman is of a few days and full of trouble.'

We cause some of the trouble we face and it is avoidable. That is to say, much, if not most of the troubles we face each day is trouble we have brought upon ourselves.

One area we bring trouble upon ourselves is in the physical area. Most of the time we have people who have physical problems say, 'I don't know why God allows me to have all these physical problems?' When they know full well their blood vessels are stopped up because they have eaten the wrong things and haven't gotten the proper exercise.

Another area of trouble we bring on ourselves is in the area of finances. People go and buy all they can afford, then go and buy the things they can't afford. They get themselves so deep in debt that they are constantly paying bills that are overdue.

Then I'm told that there are some clergy and church folk who spend a lot of hard earned cash on the lottery and at the casinos.

Some trouble is avoidable. Of course, some of the trouble we face is unavoidable.

Often trouble comes to Christians that they had nothing to do with causing. For example – children cannot control the kind of homes they are born into. Some children are born to wicked parents and it takes a lifetime for them to recover from some of the things they were exposed to as children.

People cannot help when a loved one goes home to be with the Lord and they are left behind with a broken heart. Where we are today is the result of where we were yesterday, and where we will be tomorrow is being determined by where we are today.

The text reads, 'many are the afflictions of the righteous but the Lord delivereth him out of them all.'

Some trouble is avoidable and some trouble unavoidable.

That's how it is down here. If it's not one thing, it's another.

Three things I'm going to say about Trouble and I'm through.

Can I tell you first – trouble, no one likes it, no one is successful in avoiding it, **TROUBLE SEEMS TO BE ONE OF THE FACTS OF LIFE.**

Trouble has no age preference. It invades the life of a young person as well as the old. Trouble has no respect for gender, race or social circle. Trouble invades the life of the rich and the famous.

Trouble is as inevitable as a rainy day after you have washed and polished your car. Trouble like crosses, comes in many shapes and sizes. As soon as you get your car paid for, it's falling apart. Get your car problems solved, the house problems begin. Get the roof replaced and discover that termites are eating away the foundation. If it's not the paint, it's the plumbing.

Our bodies cause us trouble. If it's not your lungs, it's your kidneys. If it's not your hair that's falling out, your teeth need fixing. If your back is not hurting, your feet are giving you trouble. If arthritis don't stop you from walking, laryngitis will stop you from talking. **If it's not one thing, it's another.**

Trouble, no one likes it, no one is successful in avoiding it. It seems to be just one important fact of life.

My second thought is **WHY GOD ALLOWS TROUBLE TO COME TO US.**

God allows trouble to come to us for many reasons. Time will permit me to mention but a few.

Trouble makes us appreciate our blessings. God wants us to appreciate the good things of life He has provided for us. The best way He can do that is to let us be exposed to some bad things too. Sometimes trouble is a blessing in disguise.

<u>Trouble makes us know that we are living a godly life.</u> Paul told his son Timothy in the Gospel ministry, 'yea, all who will live godly in Christ will suffer persecution,' and he didn't say 'maybe' or 'perhaps,' he said, 'they shall suffer persecution.'

<u>Trouble can be a blessing in disguise.</u> God always knows what is best for us. Sometimes the best for us is disguised as trouble. It may hurt for a while, but later we are able to thank God for it.

This brings me to my last part of this message.

WHERE TO GO AND WHERE TO LOOK WHEN TROUBLE COMES

I have already stated we all get in trouble and when we get in trouble we immediately look for a way or ways to get out of the trouble we find ourselves in.

I heard a country preacher say when I was a child, 'don't you trouble trouble until trouble troubles you.' I really don't know to this day what he meant by that, I guess he was telling us, as youngsters, to stay out of trouble.

But the question is, where do you go and where do you look when trouble comes? I think I need to tell us when in trouble, where you look makes a big difference.

Can I tell you, when you are in trouble, there are three directions you can look for help? When in trouble and you need help, I would suggest that you first **LOOK WITHIN**.

We need to discover when in trouble we really aren't alone. One of the names for God is Immanuel which means

God with us. There is a song that we used to sing during my childhood days, 'Something Within.' It goes: "I met God one morning, my soul feeling bad, heart heavy laden, I had a bowed down head. He lifted my burden and made me feel good. All I know, it was something within."

Where to look when trouble comes – look within.

Another direction to look when trouble comes is **Look Around**.

When I look around me, I realize I'm blessed. When you look around you see folk far worse that yourself and you count your blessings.

When in trouble, look within, look around but most of all, **LOOK UP**.

I read about a woman who at work received a call about how her daughter was very sick and needed her medications. The woman left her job, stopped by the druggist, picked up the medicine. When she got back to the car she discovered she had locked her keys in the car.

She called home and the person looking after her daughter told her to find a coat hanger and use it to open the door.

She found a coat hanger but really didn't know how to use it. She did know how to pray. So she cried out to God for help. Within five minutes time a man driving an old model rusty car saw her plight and said, 'Ma'am, look like you are in trouble. I'll help you.' Her thoughts were, is this the best God can send to help me?

In desperation she said to herself, 'what can I say but be thankful.' That man, within two minutes, took that coat hanger and opened that door. She hugged the man, thanked him and said, 'you are such a nice man.' He said, 'thanks for the compliment. I am not what you would call a nice man. I just got out of prison about two hours ago for car theft.'

The woman hugged the man again. Then loudly thanked God saying, 'Lord, you didn't just send me help, you sent me a professional.'

God is always there where you need Him. Believers should have a quiet time with the Lord every day.

I've said when in trouble, **LOOK WITHIN – LOOK AROUND – LOOK UP** and I close by saying, when in trouble **LOOK AHEAD**.

There are always better days ahead.

Trouble don't last always.

Keep traveling this road – around turns.

When you cross the river, your road is going to change.

Picked Out To Be Picked On

*"Yea and all that will live godly in Christ
Jesus shall suffer persecution."
~ II Timothy 3:12 ~
(KJV)*

*"Many are the afflictions of the righteous;
but the Lord delivereth him out of them all."
~ Psalm 34:19 ~
(NKJV)*

I remember with much gratitude many important ideas I gained while a student in a class of preaching during my Seminary days. Someone asked the late Dr. S. L. McDowell, our Homiletics professor, to give us at least one rule for us to keep our sermons up to date.

His reply was, "Remember young men, every time you preach, in your congregation there is someone with a broken heart." That was the sensible advice he gave to us more than, at least, half a century ago.

If that professor was here today, his advice would probably be so much different. He probably would say,

'Remember young men to keep your sermons up to date. Keep this in mind – there will be someone with a broken heart on every pew.'

Suffering, trouble, trials and tribulations are just some of life's inevitables for everyone. It often seems like those who try to be good and do good are forced to travel a very rough and rocky road. Few things are more frustrating than seeing rogues go free while good people suffer.

You do what you know to be the right thing and everything turns sour with you; while all around you there are folks who aren't trying to do the right thing because there's no 'do right' in them and things appear sweet and easy for them.

You play the game according to the rules and get kicked out of the game while others break every rule in the book and keep right on playing often to become the star of the team and awarded the biggest trophy.

Rogues get away with everything and you can't get away with anything. The hard hit get hit harder, the protected gets more protection.

I often ask the question when some unusual problem is squeezing me, "Lord, why?" The answer quickly comes to me like the peal of a bell on a clear night. **That's how it is down here. If it's not one thing, it's another.**

The Divine Spirit has given me the answer. Paul tells his son Timothy in the Gospel ministry, "Yea and all who will live godly in Christ Jesus shall suffer persecution." And the Psalmist writes, 'Many are the afflictions of the righteous, etc.'

My subject tonight is, **PICKED OUT TO BE PICKED ON.**

Note first when you give yourself to God and He accepts you as His child, **YOU WILL BE PICKED ON.**

There is a reason or reasons for this. The kingdom of this world is essentially at war with the Kingdom of God. Therefore, when God accepts you as His child, you are picked out to be picked on.

One of the outstanding qualities of Jesus was his sheer honesty. He never left anyone in doubt as to what would happen to them if they chose to follow Him. Jesus made it clear that He came not to make life easy, but to make men great.

The early believers, many times, had to make a choice between loyalty and living. Every time their choice was loyalty. The penalties many of the early believers had to pay were terrible beyond description. They were often flung to lions, or burned at a stake. These were kindly deaths compared to some.

Once you said, "I believe," once you decided to walk in the Jesus Way, once you decided to do God's will and serve for His glory, **You Are Picked Out To Be Picked On.**

Secondly, I call your attention to this well known fact, **THE DEVIL PICKS ON THE BEST PEOPLE.**

The devil doesn't pick on the worst folks. He picks on the best folk.

Job is a good example. Job was picked out to be picked on. The Bible tells us that he was righteous, yet he received tragic losses, defeats, disasters, calamities and all kinds of evil. Yet he affirmed a positive faith where it says when he lost his possessions, 'naked came I unto this world and naked shall I return. Though he slay me, yet will I trust Him. I know my Redeemer lives. All the days of my appointed time, I'll wait until my change comes.'

There were the Hebrew young men in the fiery furnace. These men heard their king say to them, 'bow or burn.' They said to the king, 'we will not stoop at standing time.'

John the Baptist lost his head by Herod. John the Apostle was placed on the Isle of Patmos. Stephen was stoned to death. John F. Kennedy was riffled to death in Dallas. Martin L. King, Jr. met his death in Memphis because he believed and taught that freedom is not free, that equality and justice is never surrendered voluntarily by the oppressor, it must be demanded by the oppressed, it must be demanded by the oppressed. If you don't push, nothing moves.

Above all, there was Jesus, the matchless Son of God who hung, bled and died on an old rugged cross. The devil doesn't pick on the worst folk, he picks on the best.

My third and final thought is this – **DON'T GET UPSET THAT YOU ARE PICKED OUT TO BE PICKED ON...**

... because you are given the supreme opportunity to show your loyalty to Jesus Christ.

Nowadays, it's hard to get and keep dedicated officers and leaders in the church. Somebody is always picking on them. We wonder why churches aren't growing as they should, members spend too much time picking on one another.

If Jesus was among us today, I fear He would tell church folks to pick up your cross and follow me daily, and you'll have less time picking on one another.

Pick up your cross. Don't waste your time picking on the cross-bearers. When you are picked out to be picked on, it's useless to fret and complain. Remember, God is still running this business. He rules, guides and directs the affairs of men.

Look at Pharaoh's army at the Red Sea. Look at what happened to Haman who picked on Ester, he was hanged on the gallows. He lived for one even though it seemed to be against him.

Look at what happened when they picked on Jesus. They killed Him. They buried Him in a borrowed tomb, but He rose triumphant and lives forever for His Saints to proclaim. Life is not fair but God is good.

I often tell about a man who lost his job. He had bills to pay and a family to support. He had very little left in his savings account. He didn't know when or where he would find work to do. One question that was uppermost in his mind was, 'Lord, why did this happen to me?'

Because he had nothing better to do, he decided to go for a walk in the neighborhood. While walking he came to a construction site where they were building a new church. He stood there several minutes and watched a man knocking the rough edges off some stones before he placed them in the building. He asked the workman to explain to him what was going on. The man said, "I'm shaping it down here so it will fit up there."

I'm going to close this sermon telling us, **WHEN YOU ARE PICKED OUT TO BE PICKED ON,** put the promises of God to work, stand on the promises of God. God has promised and provided so much, but we settle for so little. No promise of God will work unless we do. God specialized in making the impossible possible.

I read an account of a church in a small town in New Jersey. This church faced an insurmountable problem (at least the members thought so). They had built a new sanctuary on a recently acquired eight acre property, half of which was mountain and wilderness.

The City authorities wouldn't permit them to occupy their new building until a sufficient number of parking spaces were provided or installed. Their problem was forty feet of mountain rose up abruptly at the rear of the church leaving very little space for a parking lot to be installed. The cost to move the mountain was too much. What were they to do?

Trustees are supposed to have the answers. But, 'when the going gets tough, the tough get going.' Everyone asked the preacher, 'what are we going to do?'

The preacher read to the congregation Matthew 17:20 that reads, "If you have the faith as a grain of a mustard seed, ye shall say to this mountain remove hence to yonder place and nothing shall be impossible to you."

The old preacher said, 'Let's stand on the promises of God.' He said, 'If you believe what I read, meet me at the regular hour of prayer; let's put this matter entirely into the hands of God. Let's trust, let's work, and let's pray for the mountain to move.'

While they were praying, God was already at work. The next morning following the prayer session the phone rang. It was an executive from a phone company. They were planning to erect a new building in a large nearby swampy sight. They needed land-fill material, like sand and rocks.

They had heard of their plight and within a month this company had hauled off forty square feet of mountain for which they had paid the church $5,400.00. They not only moved the mountain, they leveled the ground for the parking lot.

The Lord knows the way through the wilderness. All we need to do is trust Him.

By and by when the morning comes....

About the Author

DR. GEORGE CALVIN MCCUTCHEN, SR.

George Calvin McCutchen, Sr., was born in Rockfield, Kentucky, March 1. 1927. He is a graduate of Tennessee A&I State University, Nashville; received his Bachelor of Theology degree from the American Baptist College of the Bible, Nashville, Tennessee; and has done graduate work at the University of Tulsa, Oklahoma. In 1974 he received the Doctorate of Divinity from the Simmons Bible College, Louisville, Kentucky. He also was awarded a Doctorate of

Divinity degree from the Jackson Theological Seminary-Shorter College, Little Rock, Arkansas; and a Doctorate of Humane Letters from Tennessee Baptist College, Memphis, Tennessee. In May of 2004, he was awarded a Doctorate of Humane Letters from the T. Oscar Chappelle Oklahoma School of Religion and a Doctorate of Letters from Phillips Theological Seminary becoming the first African-American Minister to be so honored.

Dr. McCutchen served as Assistant Pastor of Mt. Zion Baptist Church from 1953-1056, and Director of the Baptist Educational Center, Tulsa, from 1956-57. In October 1957, he returned to Mt. Zion and served as Pastor for 50 years.

Dr. McCutchen is a lecturer and an evangelist, has traveled extensively in the United States, Jamaica, West, Central, and South Africa; the Bahamas, Israel, and the Philippines.

The author of several booklets designed to build and strengthen spiritual growth. He has written publications for the Oklahoma Baptist State Convention; had sermons published in the *National Baptist Pulpit*; writes a weekly article – "Just Thinking," in *The Oklahoma Eagle.*

He is the founder of Barnabus Christian Ministries which publishes several of his workbooks, pamphlets and sermons to assist ministers (both young and seasoned) in their work and services to their congregations.

Dr. McCutchen is involved in many phases of community and denominational work. He serves as Supervisor of Young People's Leaders' Division, National Baptist Congress of Christian Education (an Auxiliary of the National Baptist Convention USA, Inc.); Past President of the Oklahoma Missionary Baptist State Convention, and the Oklahoma Baptist School of Religion; past lecturer, Creek District Baptist Pastors; lecturer, First United Baptist District Association Pastors, and the Christian Ministers Alliance.

Presently, Dr. McCutchen is the Pastor Emeritus of the Mt. Zion Baptist Church in addition to serving on several community boards. He is the Senior Advisor for the First United Baptist District Association, and a member of the City of Tulsa's Ethics Commission, a position to which he was appointed in 2006 under Mayor Kathy Taylor.

Pastor McCutchen officially retired on his anniversary date of November 11, 2007 after serving at his "one and only church" for fifty years. In honor of his retirement and long service as Pastor at Mt. Zion, his life story and several of his favorite sermons were published in a book entitled *"One of the Whosoevers."*

For 60 years, Dr. McCutchen was married to the late Adelene McCutchen.

History Of The Annual Sermon, "If It's Not One Thing, It's Another"

The late Rev. J. H. Dotson pastured the Mt. Zion Baptist Church in Tulsa, Oklahoma for 20 years retiring for health reasons. He then served as Pastor Emeritus from 1958 until 1963.

As a memorial tribute to Rev. Dotson, Dr. McCutchen established the J. H. Dotson Memorial Scholarship because of Rev. Dotson's dedicated, conscientious leadership and because of his love and interest in the academic achievements of young people.

In 2007, the Joint Board voted to enhance the name of the scholarship fund to include that of Dr. G. Calvin McCutchen, Sr. to honor him for his service and commitment to the youth of the church, community and state. The scholarship is now known as the Dotson-McCutchen Educational Foundation.

Dr. McCutchen first delivered this sermon, "If It's Not One Thing It's Another" on Sunday, July 1, 1984 at Mt. Zion Baptist Church and since that date he has delivered this message as far East as Brooklyn, New York and as far South as Jackson,

Mississippi. The theme remains the same and the message is always fresh and applicable to today's times!

This annual sermon has been delivered in conjunction with the drive for the J.H. Dotson Memorial Scholarship Fund and has been associated with the beginning of the Five Star Fellowship Revival.

Since 1995, 46 students have received scholarships and stipends to assist with college expenses. Total monies awarded, $58,900.00:

MT. ZION J.H.DOTSON
SCHOLARSHIP RECIPIENTS

1995

Denisha Johnson - Langston University
Mica Harding - Missouri State University
Freida Latimer - Tulsa University

1996

Jason Caddy - Oklahoma University
Kemper Johnson - Oklahoma University
Alicia Johnson - Oklahoma University
Erika Parks - Oklahoma University
Antonio Jeffrey - Howard University
Valesha Johnson - Florida State University

1997

Dwayne Gardner - Oklahoma State University
Melvin Wilson - Northeastern OK A&M University

Angela Williams - Clark College

1998

Rev. Victor Latimer, Jr. - Oklahoma State University
Kristin Miller - Oklahoma University
Keith Johnson - Oklahoma University

1999

Eric Ezell - Oklahoma University
Lee Gardner - Oklahoma State-Okmulgee
Latoya Lazenby - Northeastern State University
Kimberly Black - Texas Southern University
Stewart Alexander - Grambling State University

2000

Jermel Treadwell - Langston University

2001

Kyle Caddy - University of Arkansas
Dana Harding - Tulsa Community College
Shirann Johnson - Oklahoma University
Wayne Latimer - Northeastern State University
Ashley Oulds - Oklahoma University

2002

Blair Johnson - Xavier University
Brandi Cathy - University of Central Oklahoma

2003

Wendell Peters, Jr. - Northern Oklahoma College
Cameo Boyd - Northeastern Oklahoma A&M
Aaron Humphrey - Paul Quinn College

2004

Kimberly Latimer - Northeastern Oklahoma A&M
Cynthia Williams - Tulsa Community College
Kardae Richardson - Tulsa Community College
Gabrielle Alexander - Grambling State University
Rebecca Driver - Prairie View University

2005

No Mt. Zion High School Graduates

2006

Robert Johnson - Technology Center

2007

No Mt. Zion High School Graduates

2008

Kaysee Johnson - Oklahoma University
Lauren James - Tulsa Community College
Aaron Thomas - West Minister College
Megan Baccus

2009 - 2010

No Mt. Zion High School Graduates

2011

Cyndi Johnson - University of Central Oklahoma
Dominique Sells- Oklahoma State University
Melvin Murdock - Texas Southern University
Edward Boyd - Tulsa Community College
Tayla Boyd - Tulsa Community College

2012-2013

No Mt. Zion High School Graduates

CPSIA information can be obtained at www.ICGtesting.com
Printed in the USA
LVOW11s1334051014

407315LV00001B/1/P